This Book
provided by the
Pat & Elizabeth Best
Book Fund

The
BIRDCAGE
BOOK

ANTIQUE BIRDCAGES
FOR THE
CONTEMPORARY COLLECTOR

LESLIE GARISTO

Simon & Schuster

New York   London   Toronto   Sydney   Tokyo

A RUNNING HEADS BOOK

SIMON AND SCHUSTER
Simon & Schuster Building
Rockefeller Center
1230 Avenue of the Americas
New York, N.Y. 10020

SIMON AND SCHUSTER and colophon are registered trademarks
of Simon & Schuster Inc.

THE BIRDCAGE BOOK
was conceived and produced by
Running Heads Incorporated
55 West 21 Street
New York, New York 10010

Editor: Rose K. Phillips
Designer: Liz Trovato
Managing Editor: Jill Hamilton
Production Manager: Peter J. McCulloch
Endpaper illustrations by Linda Winters

10   9   8   7   6   5   4   3   2   1

Library of Congress Cataloging-in-Publication Data

Garisto, Leslie.
      The birdcage book : antique birdcages for the contemporary
collector / Leslie Garisto.
          p.   cm.
      "A Running Heads book."
      Includes index.
      ISBN 0-671-74445-3
      1. Birdcages—Collectors and collecting.   I. Title.
NK3855.G37   1992
749.3—dc20   91-759
                     21t   CIP

Typeset by Trufont Typographers Inc.
Color separations by Hong Kong Scanner Craft Company, Ltd.
Printed and bound in Singapore by Tieh Wah Press (Pte.) Ltd.

DEDICATION

For Emma, cageless bird

ACKNOWLEDGMENTS

This book—and my experience in writing it—would certainly have been the poorer without the help of many people. For their willingness to share their time and knowledge, I thank Betty Jane Bart, Jean Voight, Hethèa Nye, Howard Kaplan, John Rosselli, Marilyn Hannigan, Susan Parrish, Susan Colley, Jeanne Stueber, Jennifer Buya, Diane Blomquist, Charles Faudree, Guy Veroli, Don Black, and Danielle Kisluk-Grosheide of the Metropolitan Museum of Art. Special thanks to Tim Sullivan of the Cooper-Hewitt Library for his inspired assistance, Frederika Biggs for graciously inviting me into her home, and Betsy Nestler for being especially generous with her time. I must also thank Mary Forsell, for being a smart and gentle editor, and Andrew Baseman for his visual acuity and hard work in gathering illustrative material for the book. Thanks, always, to my husband, John—for everything. And finally, great thanks to Marta Hallett and Ellen Milionis for their friendship and support, above and beyond.

CONTENTS

Introduction

THE APPEAL
OF CAGES

An elegant nineteenth-century French birdcage and a diminutive Japanese cricket cage are both graceful and airy, qualities sought by collectors since the Victorian era. Here they complement a tablescape of bibelots and everlastings.

irdcages have inspired artisans and delighted bird-keepers for centuries. There is something about the requisite form, the necessary *airiness* of birdcages, that gives them an essential beauty. Even unadorned, they seem more ethereal than functional. Embellished, they can be fanciful, whimsical, or—at their best—exquisite. Though the Victorians were the first birdcage collectors, the hobby of bird-keeping and the craft of cage-making are probably as old as civilization itself.

We know that the ancient Greeks kept sparrows, magpies, and starlings as house pets, and during the heyday of the Roman Senate, talking parrots were all the rage. Ostensibly among the spoils of war transported from Egypt by the emperor Augustus was a raven trained to repeat "Ave, Caesar Victor Imperator!" The Chinese, whose birdcages remain among the most beautiful ever created, were making cages as early as the third century, as evidenced by these melancholy lines from a poem by Tso Ssu:

Flap, flap, the captive bird in the cage
Beating its wings against the four corners.

And during the Middle Ages, men of wealth were entertained by pet magpies, which were usually given license to fly unfettered about the house. (Chaucer refers to caged birds in "The Squire's Tale," but he may have been thinking of fowl in fattening pens.) The Renaissance ushered in not just a frenzy for exotic avian species, which made their way to European ports in the hulls of the great trading ships, but for cages as well, clearly a necessity in palaces that featured expensive rugs and upholstered furniture.

Virtually none of these cages has survived, though a more enduring representation of an early birdcage can be found on a tomb dating from 1630 in St. Andrew's Church, Norwich, England. Built for the parents of the poet Sir John Suckling, the tomb includes a square birdcage carved in stone; poised just outside it is a newly freed bird, symbolizing the release of the spirit. The cage itself is a rather prosaic affair, small, boxy, and unornamented, but we know that roomy and appealing wicker cages were in wide use at the time, especially in the Netherlands, since they appear frequently in the works of seventeenth-century Dutch painters, from Vermeer to Rembrandt. The French, too, were establishing themselves as cage-makers; indeed, France was the only nation to boast a royally chartered cage-makers guild. But it

The clean, geometric lines and soaring verticality of this brass-wire cage make it the dramatic focal point of a traditional living room.

wasn't until the eighteenth century that the art of cage-making saw its first great inflorescence.

Suddenly, no great house could be constructed without an aviary, and no man or woman of fashion could resist the temptation of an ornately carved cage. Both Louis XV and Louis XVI commissioned elaborate cages that were placed among the orange trees in the garden at Versailles. For the first time in history, the cage itself began to take precedence over the bird inside. This was, in fact, the era of the birdless cage: from thumbnail-size porcelain min-

This British dining room evokes a Dickensian "curiosity shop" air. The two-story word-and-wire cage, complete with winged resident, adds a lively element to the visual potpourri.

iatures into which no bird could possibly fit to gorgeously decorative cages built for mechanical songsters. Also popular at the time were delicate statuettes incorporating birdcages, of Meissen porcelain and Staffordshire china.

By the nineteenth century, the birdcage had become almost an essential furnishing in well-to-do homes across Europe. Under Napoleon III, the French produced birdcages that were wonders of miniature architecture, and the rest of Europe followed suit. Behind turreted walls and balustered windows, it was sometimes nearly impossible to spot the birds inside. But the cages were glorious.

The English took the mania for cages to new heights. By century's end, no middle-class English parlor was without its pet budgerigar, and in the houses of the wealthy, an extravagant birdcage was likely to be the centerpiece of the drawing room. At midcentury, birdcage replicas of the Crystal Palace were in great demand, and wirework Taj Mahals reminded bird fanciers that the sun set neither on the Empire nor on its feathered pets. Perhaps it was the popularity of birdcages that inspired designers of wicker furniture to give their chairs and settees what were commonly called "birdcage legs."

Nineteenth-century Americans were equally enamored of birdcages, which replicated everything from native American buildings to sailing vessels. Some of the most handsome cages of the time were designed by Calvert Vaux and Jacob Wrey Mould to line the bucolic walkways of New York's Central Park.

In addition to their physical beauty, birdcages have long exerted a powerful symbolic appeal. In virtually every culture, the bird has been a metaphor for the human soul; the birdcage, in turn, represented the corporeal prison of the soul. Shakespeare's plays abound with birdcage references, one of the most quoted being Rosalind's comparison, in *As You Like It,* of a man ensnared by love to "a bird confined in a cage of rushes." Understandably, a cage with an open door was a popular symbol of escape. Perhaps the most intriguing symbolic use of the birdcage was made by those inveterate cage-makers the Dutch, for whom the caged bird represented chastity. The virtue of a young woman holding an empty cage in a Dutch painting is highly suspect.

In the twentieth century, the fashion for birdcages has ebbed and flowed. Home design magazines of the thirties advanced the notion of the "bird room," which was to be equipped with fountains and spacious aviaries, and mass manufacturers of the era turned out appealing reproductions of historic cages. But by the fifties, cages had for the most part lost their decorative function. Then, in the 1980s, a confluence of factors—Postmodernism, a wave of Anglophilia, and a renewed interest in recycling old objects—helped spark a renaissance for the cage as decorative accessory. Once again, the form itself became visually compelling, and has been represented in everything from Mario Buatta's needlepoint pillow-cage and Tiffany's new Audubon china pattern to Isabel Canovas's arresting birdcage earrings. In the pages that follow, birdcages from all eras exhibit their aesthetic resiliency and undeniable charm. There is something immensely appealing about having a birdcage around the house. Perhaps it's the classic beauty of a richly embellished eighteenth-century mahogany dome, or the fantasy of a wood-and-wire Swiss chalet. Or it might be the soft patina of weathered paint on an old tin cage. Tenanted or not, the birdcage reminds us of our connection to the natural world, and compels us, for a little while at least, to forget the ponderous and the earthbound.

One of the many delights of birdcages is their versatility. Here, a domed brass cage, suspended from the ceiling of a collectible-filled sitting room, draws the eye upward—and outward, to the view beyond the mullioned glass door.

Chapter One

RUSTICS

A finch nesting in a dome of painted wire, a magpie in a rough-hewn bentwood cage, a wild songbird in wickerwork—these may well have been history's first real pets. Dogs and cats were domesticated earlier, but they were less pets than servants, kept mainly for hunting and rodent killing. As early as 600 B.C., when the Chinese were domesticating cormorants for fishing, the biblical prophet Jeremiah referred to "a cage filled with birds." Though Jeremiah may have been speaking of a fattening pen for domesticated fowl, the wicker cages of ancient Pompeii, which numbered among its commercial establishments a thriving aviary, surely housed birds kept only for the pleasure of their plumage and the immeasurable joy of their song.

For the Roman nobility, according to Cicero, caged birds signified a prosperous domesticity. And by the Middle Ages, the keeping of birds was an established pastime of the aristocratic leisure class. In the days of stone floors and minimal furnishings, many of those birds were allowed to fly throughout medieval interiors. But Chaucer's mention in "The Squire's Tale" of "briddes . . . that men in cases fede" stands as literary proof that some bird-keepers were more fastidious.

No illustrations of these early cages survive, but they were undoubtedly less decorative than functional, made of the materials we still associate with the rustic—bamboo, twig, reed, bent osier (a kind of

A weathered wooden birdcage is right at home amid the tropical plantings on this California patio. Cages with a rustic appearance work particularly well in an outdoor setting.

willow), sturdy wood of all kinds, and later, metal wire. Even in the golden age of European cage-making, which reached its apogee during the reign of Napoleon III (from 1852 to 1871), rustic cages were being produced in great numbers throughout Europe, to hang from the eaves of countless country cottages, as they still do today. And far from the court of Napoleon, peasant craftsmen in Mexico, South America, and Asia were creating traditional birdcages that remain the inspiration for many of today's imported designs.

Because they were fashioned of perishable materials, most of these cages succumbed to the abuses of time and their spirited inhabitants. Collectors are far more likely to come across an elaborately architectural nineteenth-century French cage than a simple rustic cage from the same period—not just because the rustics were more fragile but because they were less treasured.

Today, of course, rustic style is appreciated for the very simplicity that once made it an object of aesthetic scorn. There is something irresistible about a simple domed cage of unpainted wicker or a small square country cage whose battered wire and splintered wood tell a story of use and age. Even those most basic of rustic cages—chicken coops and fattening pens—exert a singular if ironic charm.

An olive-green painted-wood cage nestles comfortably beneath a twig bench, adding an additional note of whimsy to this fanciful indoor "garden."

19

QUOTIDIAN CAGES

A surprising variety of rustic cages is available to the collector. In addition to coops, which can sometimes be found abandoned along country roads or picked up for a song in rural thrift shops, there are market cages designed, as their name suggests, to display birds for sale, or to carry birds to and from the market. The simplest of these are large, unpainted wooden cages, square or rectangular, still used in many rural markets around the world; the carrying cages are generally smaller, with wooden or wood-and-wire handles, and were more likely to belong to the housewife than the farmer.

Grouped together, prosaic wooden cages have the feeling of sculpture. Simple lines, muted colors, and a patina of use add to their country-style charm.

A distant cousin is the carrier-pigeon cage, which was typically made almost entirely of wood with delicate, turned columns instead of wiring, and a textile cover. Though rare, these functional but elegant cages do turn up in antiques shops and flea markets from time to time. One of the most graceful market cages was meant to house a single dove, or perhaps a pair: made entirely of bent twig, it was conical in shape, tapering at the top to resemble a rustic Eiffel Tower.

Rustic doesn't necessarily mean un-adorned, as evidenced by the intricate lines of this bamboo cage. Vernacular architectural cages like this one have been made in the Philippines for well over a century.

ARCHITECTURAL RUSTICS

Some rustic cages were decidedly architectural. A nineteenth-century visitor to the Channel Islands described osier blackbird cages hanging outside peasant cottages; they resembled nothing more, he said, than "the wattled houses of the ancient Celts." A rare nineteenth-century cage from the Azores features several wings, semicircular arches suggesting doors or windows, and a conical roof topped with a small wooden finial, recalling the design of a typical Spanish cathedral. A cage from the same era but hailing from the Philippines is of similar construction, but its more delicate bamboo lends itself to graceful curves and gives the cage a surprising delicacy and airiness.

Most rustic cages, however, were unornamented, except perhaps for an application of paint. A popular—and appealing—antique rustic is the domed linnet cage. Abundant in the nineteenth-century French countryside, these cages for linnets and other wild finches were typically of painted wirework, twelve to fifteen inches high, and topped with suspension hooks. (Reproductions are plentiful, so collectors should be especially wary when presented with an "authentic" period linnet cage.) Square wood-and-wire cages were also painted, usually in vivid colors to contrast with dimly lit interiors, and

Inexpensive rustic cages, crafted in Mexico, are transformed by the application of paint.

some of these have managed to survive to this day with paint intact.

A drawing of a birdcage-maker's shop in Seville that appeared in a 1902 issue of *Century* magazine wonderfully illustrates the typical rustic cages of the time. Stacked by the curb are several large rectangular market cages. Above the doorway hang three simple domed cages, perhaps of wood, and against the whitewashed wall are several dozen simple, square cages of wire, some diminutive, others roomier, depending on their intended tenants. A few of these cages were designed to be used as traps; hung on an exterior wall, they were baited (sometimes with their domesticated cousins) to attract wild birds. Today, collectors occasionally echo history by mounting cages on the rusticated walls of country houses.

Other rustic cages made their way to Europe on trading ships beginning in the sixteenth century. One

In a farmhouse kitchen, above, a peaked-roof bamboo cage is the crowning touch atop a collection of pots and cooking utensils. Baskets in a variety of forms echo the cage's warp-and-weft look and make for a witty country-style tableau. Right, the wirework whorls of this contemporary cage make it undeniably decorative, but its rusted finish gives it a charming rustic feel.

of the most common nineteenth-century love-offerings from a sailor to his sweetheart was a bamboo or wire parrot cage brought back from some exotic port of call. Mexican bamboo cages were especially treasured, and one makes an appearance in no less distinguished a setting than Mozart's *The Magic Flute,* strapped to the back of Papageno. The early twentieth century's greatest collector of cages, Alexander Wilson Drake, was especially fond of a Mexican cage of reed, designed for him by an elderly peasant cage-maker; flat on two sides, it has an elegantly arched bentwood "roof" and is reminiscent of certain contemporary Mexican cages, which are now generally made of a more fragile wicker.

JAPANESE VISIONS

Perhaps the most exotic rustic cages came from Japan. In addition to wood-and-rattan cages artfully fashioned to resemble native huts, the Japanese produced numerous insect cages. Many of these were ornate, but some were simple rectilinear structures of rattan, bamboo, and unpainted wood, intended to house, among other insect pets, the kirigirisu, a kind of cricket prized for its rhythmic chirp, and esteemed as the prophet of frost. The Chinese, known primarily for the elegantly ornate cages of the eighteenth-century Ch'ien-lung period, also produced rustic cages in great number. The early-twentieth-century photographer Henri Cartier-Bresson brought back striking pictures of old men sitting with their caged birds in Peking teahouses.

Wooden cages from Mexico, painted in a variety of eye-catching colors, make the most of a basic white wall and draw the eye as effectively as any work of art.

COLLECTING RUSTICS TODAY

Today rustic cages abound, thanks largely to the booming import market. Especially decorative—and numerous—are domed wood-and-wire cages from Mexico. Their plump shape is particularly pleasing and, because of their essential simplicity (and relatively low price), they lend themselves naturally to ornamentation. They can be found colorwashed, in subtle pastels or startling shades of fuchsia and magenta, or trimmed with delicate bouquets of dried flowers. Bamboo cages imported from the Philippines are also popular. Simpler than their nineteenth-century predecessors, they are often equally architectural in design.

Whether a genuine antique or a reproduction, the rustic cage has sparked the imagination of many a collector. Some group dozens on shelves or in bookcases. Others use them alone as unexpected accents. Diane Blomquist, whose Maryland country house overflows with cages from a variety of periods, has one large market cage tucked surprisingly under a kitchen table. And a Denver couple used a weathered chicken coop to spectacular effect in their kitchen. Mounted high on the wall to disguise an air vent, it features an ersatz chicken atop real straw; dangling from the coop are bunches of dried flowers and two trompe l'oeil whimsies: a pheasant ready for plucking and a roped bouquet of garlic.

The traditional half-sun motif gets a new twist in an elaborate rusted-wire cage. The wire stand takes the cage from the realm of the rustic to the regal.

The earliest cage-makers created unpretentious objects for everyday men and women who sought to introduce a small element of the wild into the domestic landscape. Though their primary aim was to manufacture a functional rather than a beautiful product, they certainly brought skill and an artisan's sensibility to their work, not to mention an affinity for the objects of their craftsmanship. (Every commercial cage-maker had at least one songbird of his own, displayed prominently by the front door of his establishment.) It is undoubtedly that affinity we feel today when we are drawn to a weather-worn willow cage in the window of an urban antiques shop. We may no longer seek to fill our cages with living birds, but those cages continue to represent a bit of nature, nestled comfortably under the eaves.

Left, the pleasing gradations of color on a well-worn wood-and-wire cage add to its appeal—and its value. The cage's plump, rounded shape echoes the lines of the bowed corner cabinet below it. Above, designer Mark Osborne drew on the half-timbered architecture of New England barns to create this rustic-style aviary.

Chapter Two

CLASSICS

*I*n the making of birdcages, form hasn't always followed function. The nineteenth century in particular was given to wild excesses of ornamentation; Victorian and other nineteenth-century cages are as likely to resemble Venetian palaces or Gothic cathedrals as domiciles for birds. All cages, of course, have certain design prerequisites: they need bars of some sort to keep their flighty inhabitants inside, but they must be open enough so that prize specimens can be viewed from the outside. Beyond this, as history has demonstrated, anything goes, from turrets to towers to anthropomorphic wirework.

Flat-backed cages, mounted against a wall, turn a hallway into a whimsical gallery. The garden motif of the main room is echoed in the ivy garlands that twine around the cages' wirework.

Nevertheless, as in all aspects of the decorative arts, there are certain classic designs in which use and beauty merge with a minimum of fuss and fancy. These are the cages designed as much for the bird within as the ogler without, and yet the best are as pleasing to the eye as any nineteenth-century confection. Ranging from simple Early American domes of wood and wire to meticulously carved Chinese cages of ivory and tortoiseshell, all are functional and each in its own way is beautiful.

EARLY CAGES

Decorative birdcages were being made as early as the fourteenth century in Europe. Among a 1380 inventory of the possessions of Charles V are listed several birdcages ornamented with gemstones, and in 1450, a good four decades before she financed Columbus, Queen Isabella paid an artist forty pieces of pewter to paint her birdcages. Around the same time, Louis XI was decorating his salon with birds in cages, one of which was described as having a silver base painted with scenes of country life. While these royal cages were far from rustic, they were most likely simple in basic design, despite their sometimes opulent ornamentation.

The best of the early cages were of French or Dutch origin. Indeed, for the French, bird-catching and cage-making were the exclusive province of roy-

This brass cage from England dates from the middle of the nineteenth century. Classic in form and material, it is distinguished by the unusual—and pleasing—inclination of its swirling vertical bars.

Above, in the kitchen of a Manhattan penthouse, a classic finial-topped cage is the centerpiece of a dramatic wallscape. Flat-backed cages like this were meant to be hung against a wall, where their delicate wirework can be clearly "read." Note the interesting play of light and shadow. Right, a similar cage, elevated on a stand, takes on a more formal look in this eclectic sitting room.

ally chartered guilds (*cageiolers*), which turned out a variety of classic brass- and iron-wire cages. Though the designs of the cages varied from square and squat to slender and domed, they came in two essential styles: *cages chanteresses,* which were high cages for male songbirds, and *cages muettes,* which were low cages for the quieter females, kept for breeding rather than singing. Some of the most charming cages of the period were graced with faience bases depicting rural scenes.

The Dutch were at least as prolific as the French, though in Holland cage-making was more of a cottage industry. Evidence of the Dutch fondness for birdcages abounds, most notably in the works of seventeenth-century painters like Vermeer and Jan Steen, who were clearly taken with the aesthetics of the simple but elegant cages of the era. And for prosperous Dutch burghers, birds in ivory or wooden cages were an emblem of their success as international traders.

THE EIGHTEENTH CENTURY

By the 1700s bird-keeping was all the rage among men and women of fashion in England and France. Cages à la mode reflected quality workmanship and were usually made of luxurious materials. Brass-and-mahogany cages, many of which were never intended to house living birds, were especially popular

For centuries, the Chinese have pro-duced elegant birdcages representing an unsurpassed harmony of form and function. This contemporary bamboo cage lacks the lavish accessories that distinguish the most collectible Chinese antiques, but its form and subtle orna-mentation give it a lasting charm.

among the English. Occasional examples still turn up on the auction block or in antiques shops, and be-cause they don't tend to conform to a particular architectural style, the use of mahogany is the most reliable indicator of their age and origin. One espe-cially charming English cage of the period, meant to house a skylark or two, features a bowed facade of varnished wood, faintly architectural in its resem-blance to the houses that line the streets of such quintessentially English towns as Bath and Chester.

No style is more evocative of eighteenth-century England than Chippendale, as popular for birdcages as for furniture. The graceful Chippendale cage in the Bertrand Room of Delaware's Winterthur Restoration (now available as a reproduction in the museum's catalogue) is a perfect example, with its knobbed feet and elegant pagoda-style roof. Similar cages could be found in the drawing rooms of eighteenth-century style-setters. The birds often dined more graciously in these posh cages than humans of the time, taking their seed from Sèvres porcelain bowls and sipping their water out of silver drinking troughs.

Many cages hanging in English houses of the time were of Dutch inspiration or imported. In the early part of the century these were likely to be domes of dark, varnished wood and wire, with turned baluster uprights and often with metal inlay. But as the cen-tury waned, the Dutch began producing what would become the most classic of Dutch cages: beautiful wire constructions ornamented with delftware. These began appearing around 1760; most are square or arched, with delftware bases and inserts depicting typical low-country landscapes, including windmills, ducks, boats on canals, and scenes of happy domestic life. The style was so popular, especially among the acquisitive English, that Dutch craftsmen continued to produce delftware cages into the twentieth century. One fine example of the style, dating from either the eighteenth or nineteenth century, is in the permanent collection of New York's Metropolitan Museum of Art.

A striking steel cage, crafted in France in the early part of this century, is surprisingly at home in a formal Biedermeier setting.

VICTORIAN CLASSICS

It was in the nineteenth century that keeping exotic birds was no longer the sole province of the aristocracy. Indeed, the birdcage was often the focal point of the middle-class Victorian parlor. Cage-makers' imaginations took hold, and they produced extravaganzas that were dazzlingly decorative but sometimes less than hospitable to their avian tenants.

Even in those days of ornamental excess, certain classic styles emerged, in particular the wirework birdcage. This was the golden age of the garden, as well as the dawn of mass production, and even for modest homeowners, a few pieces of wirework furniture and ornament were de rigueur for lawn and garden. These delicate-looking but surprisingly sturdy pieces—baskets, chairs, plant stands, settees, and, of course, birdcages—travelled easily from lawn to conservatory, and by midcentury countless canaries and budgerigars nested happily in homes of fanciful steel-and-iron wirework, painted in colors that harmonized with Victorian gardens. Though they derived most of their ornamentation from the delicate fretwork, some cages featured amusing accessories like revolving perches. Wirework pieces are still available to the collector, as are clever reproductions. The most telling clue to a nineteenth-century cage's authenticity is layered paint, sometimes chipping or giving way to rusty iron.

During the nineteenth century, cages topped with single or double domes abounded. They were no doubt inspired by the mansard-roof houses of Paris, where many of the cages were crafted.

Though classic in form, this dome-topped cage is more overtly architectural than most—and likely to command a higher price as well.

With the advent of mass production, attractive birdcages were available to virtually everyone, and as the century progressed they became increasingly important elements of Victorian interior design. Companies already producing small items with metal components—toy manufacturers, for example—found it easy, and lucrative, to add birdcages to their lines. By far the most famous of the mass manufacturers was the Andrew B. Hendryx Company of Lenox, Massachusetts, which began producing affordable and elegant brass cages in the late nineteenth century. The sturdy cages were manufactured in great number, and many can still be found today, at a reasonable price. (Hendryx continued producing until the 1950s, so the company name doesn't necessarily guarantee nineteenth-century vintage.) The cages' simple lines, gleaming brass, and domed shape make them for many the epitome of *birdcage*.

DECKING THE CAGE

Simplicity of style and straight-lined geometry are the hallmarks of classic cages. A sculptural model set on a table-top, left, makes this alfresco dining room even cheerier. Surrounded by forsythia blossoms, a beautifully detailed cloud-white cage makes a pleasant summer home for household birds, right.

Most classic cages, by dint of their simple lines, are particularly well suited to ornamental treatment (although any style of cage can be embellished, if you wish). Many collectors use them as planters, or group them, suspended from a sunroom ceiling, with hanging plants. A single brass cage hung from a pink ribbon graces the chintz-laden bedroom of a Victorian rowhouse in Brooklyn Heights, New York, and in a French country kitchen a simple, angular bird-cage dangles from an ornate cast-iron bracket. Betsy Nestler, an antiques dealer in New Preston, Connecticut, displays her domed brass cages grouped together on the floor, topped with moiré bows.

Jennifer Buya, a dealer in antique lace and linens, became an unwitting collector of cages when she moved to her house in a Chicago suburb. The lace curtain hanging in her dining room window let in desirable light as well as a less than desirable view of the neighboring house. Bird cages, picked up for ten dollars or less at local flea markets and painted white, seemed the perfect solution. They didn't block the light but distracted significantly from the house next door. Years later, Jennifer's passion for cages is unabated, and she sometimes drapes them with pieces of vintage lace from her own shop in Winnetka.

Diminutive wire cages made their appearance in

Airy birdcages, left, add to the drama of a light-filled, all-white kitchen. A classic domed cage in the foreground draws the eye to an oversized aviary against the far wall, where a family of songbirds happily sport. Above the table, a pagoda-style "chandelier" subtly continues the birdcage theme. Right, contemporary rattan cages in a variety of classic styles form an intriguing still life.

the nineteenth century, and these small beauties look particularly appealing as a group. New York decorator Hethèa Nye (herself an inveterate collector) hung several small cages in the window of her East Side shop, each at a different height; customers were so taken with the tableau that she could barely keep the cages in stock.

One of the most ingenious uses of classic cages is as lighting fixtures. A decade ago the Barbados-based stage designer Oliver Messel began wiring them as

Reproductions of the classic dome-topped Victorian cage abound. This one is ornamented with a sinuous garland of metal ivy.

Classic cages are distinguished by an elegant simplicity of form and subtle ornamentation, such as the finial atop this popular Victorian cage.

lanterns, and audiences were instantly enchanted.

Frederika Biggs, a decorator and collector, frequently uses birdcages as lighting fixtures, most recently in a child's bedroom, and in her Park Avenue apartment as well. She now boasts a collection of over a dozen vintage birdcages, but she bought her first one ten years ago, to use as a lamp with an "outdoorsy" feel in a dressing room she was decorating as a folly. A more elaborate birdcage serves as a surprising chandelier above her dining room table. She has also used birdcages as centerpieces, draped with ivy or festooned with boxwood swags and gold ribbon for Christmas.

Linda Steuber, a collector of birdcages and antique Christmas ornaments who lives in Tarpon Springs, Florida, displays bird ornaments in her cages during the holidays.

Classic cages lend themselves to another, more obvious use. Though antiques should be checked first for the presence of lead or jagged wires, the cages' open design, simplicity of construction, and functional shape make them the ideal indoor home for living birds.

CHINESE CAGES

The most extraordinary of classic cages were produced by Chinese artisans during the era of Ch'ien-
lung (1735–1796), a ruler known as a connoisseur
and patron of the arts. But long before, birds and
birdcages were an essential element of Chinese domestic life. Historical records dating from the third
century B.C. report that the Duke of Ch'i sent a caged
osprey as a gift to the King of Ch'u (alas, the messen-
ger was inept and the bird never reached the king),
and a proverb from the second century B.C. admon-
ishes, "If you try to put the Phoenix into a quail's
cage, the cage will not hold it, even if the Phoenix
closes its wings."

By Ch'ien-lung's reign, no family of station was
without a caged songbird, and the cages of the era
reflect not just a reverence for birds but a perfect
melding of aesthetics and function. The cages were
extremely simple in overall shape, but displayed an
enormously pleasing symmetry; most were cylindri-
cal with slightly domed "roofs." Though they were
meant to be suspended from a ceiling or doorway,
many had intricately carved openwork feet and featured beautifully wrought hooks of silver or other
precious metals. Chinese artisans used minimal decoration on the cages themselves; their real beauty
derives from the attention lavished on fittings and
materials. Some cages were of simple bamboo or

teakwood, but the better models might be tortoiseshell with bars of buffalo horn or lacquered wood with slender ivory "wires." The list of materials used to make a Ch'ien-lung cage now in the collection of New York's Cooper-Hewitt Museum evokes the essence of luxury: ebony inlaid with ivory, jade, cloisonné, amber, and porcelain.

A very basic wood-and-wire cage is lifted out of the ordinary through the inspired application of paint.

The Ch'ien-lung–era artisans reserved their most spectacular work for the cages' fittings and accessories. One cage of the period came with a carved ivory container for live worms and a matching pair of miniature ivory tongs, ivory-tipped wood perches, and a chain of amethyst and jade. Another was equipped with a carved ivory perch in the form of an old man with a crooked stick, and drinking and feeding cups fashioned to resemble a fish, a crab, and a grinning dragon. Porcelain was also common, used for water pots or small flower holders that were attached to the outside of the cages.

Quite a few cages of the Ch'ien-lung era have survived, and most are in remarkably good condition, thanks largely to the care taken by their creators and their owners. Many are in museums, but some do appear occasionally in auction catalogues. Reproductions of the basic style are quite common, though most are of unornamented bamboo or varnished wood. Because of their simplicity, many people supply ornaments of their own, ranging from beribboned rosebud pomanders to dried hydrangeas to living plants.

A popular nineteenth-century English motif, the half-sun was often incorporated into birdcage design. Mimicking the sun itself, this simple wood-and-wire cage casts a dramatic shadow.

Chapter Three

ARCHITECTURALS

*I*t's a house anyone would admire. Behind a low brick wall and imposing iron gates, a Doric colonnade flanks a bank of tall, arched windows, echoing the shape of the balustered dome that rises from the roof. Despite the crest above the entryway, this is not the home of some eighteenth-century aristocrat—though it may well have housed his songbirds. And although its intricately carved walnut body and gilded iron bars mark it as extraordinary in the realm of birdcages, it represents an abiding trend in cage design.

No doubt since the first wild bird was coaxed to sing behind bars of wicker or reed, birdcage builders have thought of their creations as houses in miniature. Early "primitive" cages from the Philippines and the Azores clearly echo the domed roofs and transepts of local houses of worship; willow cages from the Channel Islands recall the clean lines and earthy materials of Celtic wattle-and-daub architecture. Whether or not they pleased their avian tenants, these architectural cages clearly delighted both their creators and their owners—and they remain the most popular, and collectible, of cages.

Many architectural cages sacrificed airiness for detail, but this breathtaking French cage, circa 1840, deftly blends both. Its original paint adds to its collectibility.

ATTENTION TO DETAILS

This contemporary cage derives its antique feel from the inspired recycling of elements from a variety of old cages. Though entirely original in design, it harks back to the eighteenth century, when all things Chinoise were the vogue in stylish English households.

Around the turn of the century, the intrepid traveller and magazine editor Alexander Wilson Drake was amassing what remains one of the world's most impressive collections of antique birdcages (now part of the permanent collection of the Cooper-Hewitt Museum). What fascinated Drake, and so many collectors who came after him, were the architectural principles that guided the cage's creation. A writer of the time, describing Drake's collection, observed that it was easy "in many instances to trace the architectural antecedents of a people in its cage-work."

The principle continues to guide serious collectors and dealers. According to John Rosselli—a New York antiques dealer who manufactures his own line of reproduction birdcages, as well as proffering one-of-a-kind antique cages to the decorating trade—the

A twin-peaked nineteenth-century French cage is modeled after a Swiss chalet. Subtle touches include a pair of dormer windows and woodwork ornamented with a charming floral motif.

architectural details on a cage are the clearest indicators of both its age and its country of origin. Of course, for most of us, architectural influences are simply part of the irresistible charm of birdcages. Howard Kaplan, a collector since the 1970s, admits that buying birdcages satisfies his architectural urges. "It's a great deal cheaper than buying actual houses," he explains.

But even for those historical potentates who could well afford a multitude of dwellings, the miniature turrets and doorways, windows and pediments, and domes and crenellations of countless royal birdcages were the essence of charm and wit. In 1880 King Ludwig II of Bavaria commissioned an elaborately architectural cage of fruitwood, mahogany, and glass for his bedchamber in the castle of Neuschwanstein. Its intricate late Gothic carving exactly matched that of the monarch's imposingly Teutonic four-poster bed. Across the Channel, the Duke and Duchess of Bedford were taking possession of a two-tiered songbird pavilion, whose turrets and chimney stacks rivaled in resplendence the surrounding estate of Woburn Abbey.

Eighteenth-century birdcages in particular reveal a fondness for architectural embellishment. In the collection of the Philadelphia Museum is an exquisite English cage whose use of classical ornament (carved drapery swags and tiered plinth) clearly shows the influence of the brothers Adam. A similar cage, featuring a cupola and circular colonnade, is on exhibit at New York's Metropolitan Museum of Art. By far the most common feature borrowed from the world of architecture is the dome. Nineteenth- and early-twentieth-century cage-makers often enhanced simple wood-and-wire cages with the addition of a single or double dome. The combination of squared base and fluid "roof" makes these otherwise spare cages architecturally compelling. Sometimes the cages were further adorned with gilded finials or scrollwork, and many can be found today in antiques shops. This style is also extremely popular in reproduction, so it is vital to determine that a domed cage presented as antique is genuine.

During the golden age of cage-making in the nineteenth century, architectural details often obscured a cage's true function, as well as the avian inhabitants within. The cage above is a wonder of miniature architecture, with its double chimneys, dormer windows, and "brick" facade.

Architectural cages needn't replicate boxy buildings, as this dainty avian edifice demonstrates.

BUILDING ON A SMALL SCALE

Without doubt, the most spectacular architectural cages are the painstaking reproductions of buildings in miniature. These found their most exquisite expression in the second half of the nineteenth century. Even before this, however, wonders of underscale architecture were being manufactured throughout the European continent. When the fever for all things Gothic swept England in the late eighteenth century, cage-makers were quick to incorporate the style's signature arches and tracery into their own creations. A cage dating from around 1760 in the collection of H. G. Fenwick boasts a wonderful set of clerestory-style windows and typically Gothic glazing— features that were incorporated into many cages of the period. Perhaps the ultimate melding of the Gothic style and the frenzy for bird-keeping is the fabulous Gothic aviary at Strawberry Hill (the estate built for novelist Horace Walpole), itself the last word in the eighteenth-century Gothic Revival style. Other eighteenth-century cages reflect the influence of Georgian architecture. One especially appealing cage of the era is a perfect model of a Georgian house, with stacked chimneys, dormer windows, gilded cones at the eaves, and, to further the illusion of human habitation, the number 37 painted on the door.

Another eighteenth-century style that manifested itself in the cage-maker's art was Chippendale. Examples of Chippendale cages abound, but one of the most extravagant was the centerpiece of a romantic folly designed by the decorator Barbara Ostrum for the 1990 Kips Bay Boys' and Girls' Club Decorator Show House in New York City. Set against a bank of tracery windows, the cage has three pagoda-shaped towers adorned with tiny gilded bells; the arches over its "windows" and "doorway" echo the pagoda shape, and the effect overall is diaphanous and fantastic, evocative of a century that revered the exotic. Similar in effect are the Indian-style cages from the same period, some of which resemble diminutive Taj Mahals, both in form and intricacy of design.

White upholstery, an Oriental screen, and a tablecloth scattered with tiny flowers all take on a country feel when teamed with a gazebo-style birdcage. Similar cages decked many a Victorian garden and conservatory.

THE CAGE-MAKER'S GOLDEN AGE

An open porch is the perfect setting for this fanciful architectural cage, which seems to be inhaling its own breath of country air. Closer inspection reveals a careful attention to detail, including a delicate inlay of frosted glass. Birdcages harmonize naturally with garden-room furnishings, like the bent-twig chair and settee, and louvered shutters.

Victorian craftsmen and mass manufacturers alike turned out a vast array of fancifully architectural cages. Across Europe all manner of castles, gazebos, chalets, temples, churches, palaces, and pyramids were being produced to house warblers in the nineteenth-century. Some well-heeled bird owners went so far as to commission replicas of their own grand houses. Whimsy was the order of the day, reflected in turreted "Norman" castles, soaring Egyptian-style obelisks, and countless bell-towered churches. The Swiss, who for centuries had excelled as toymakers, produced glorious miniature chalets with pitched roofs and ornate balconies. American cages of the period, reflecting the vernacular architecture of the day, often resembled Hawthorne's seven-

A contemporary architectural cage blends felicitously with traditional furnishings. Like much of twentieth-century art, the cage suggests rather than mimics its source. A white finish gives the cage its clean, minimalist look.

gabled house, and cages from Quebec took their architectural cue from the typical Quebec house, with its squat chimneys, narrow windows, and steeply pitched roof.

Many cages of the era were fashioned after real buildings. French *colombiers*, large floor-standing cages that housed whole families of doves, frequently drew their inspiration from French cathedrals, and at least one, discovered by New York dealer Betty Jane Bart, was a detailed replica of Notre Dame.

But perhaps the most imitated edifice of all was the Crystal Palace, that apotheosis of Victoriana. With its vast dome of white-painted iron and glass, it resembled nothing so much as a magnificently overscale birdcage, and cage-makers produced white-painted wood-and-wire replicas by the thousands.

The French created the most fanciful and elaborate architectural birdcages, especially during the nineteenth-century reign of Napoleon III. These are the antique cages most likely to turn up in shops and at auction, and they are breathtaking in their variety. Some feature mansard-type roofs; others have soaring clock towers; still others resemble French provincial cottages.

HOUSES WITHIN HOUSES

It is no stylistic coincidence that the majority of the previous century's cages, elaborate as they may be, are flat-backed. While most eighteenth-century cages were designed to sit atop small tables, most nineteenth-century cages were intended to be mounted against a wall. (Some were actually three-sided, with wooden or mirrored backs.) Howard Kaplan displays most of his collection this way, hung at various heights against a white stucco wall in his Connecticut country house. The effect is extraordinary: the cages clearly "read" best against a stark background, which emphasizes their intricate wire-

This glorious cage would no doubt feel right at home lining a Parisian boulevard—or at least a bird-size replica of one. Among its wealth of architectural details are a shingle mansard-type roof, "brick" chimneys and trim, windows graced by balconies, and charmante painted curtains. Well-appointed birds make their entrance through elegant French doors and exercise their legs on a pair of stairways flanking the facade.

work. In her top-floor Manhattan kitchen, the decorator Frederika Biggs has hung a large cage against the wall to disguise an unsightly water valve. Mounted in this way, architectural cages become artwork in relief, as visually compelling as paintings but with a tactile quality few paintings possess.

Because of their complexity and large scale, architectural cages have the aesthetic presence to stand alone. Pamela Gaylin Ryder and Lawrence Paolantonio, designers for Pierre Deux, used a double-domed nineteenth-century cage in a French country kitchen; its graceful, clean lines seem the epitome of the French countryside. A large painting on the opposite wall complements the tableau; its subject matter includes a straw-domed aviary.

As emblems of the builder's art in miniature, architectural cages have a special place within the house, echoing the lines and embellishment of a room, or providing a startling counterpoint. Mies van der Rohe's oft-quoted architectural maxim—that God is in the details—seems especially fitting when applied to these small masterpieces, which are themselves both detail and *detailed*.

Chapter Four

FLIGHTS OF
FANCY

As in every artistic endeavor, birdcage-making has spawned its own idiosyncratic geniuses, craftsmen and purveyors who spurned the obvious and the traditional in favor of a more personal vision. Taken together, they are a patchwork lot, from the sophisticated L'Oiselier, celebrated during the reign of Louis XIV for his fabulous, gem-encrusted cages, to an anonymous Italian boy who at the turn of the century was moved to create a painstaking and extraordinary replica of Venice's Rialto Bridge out of carved wood and turned wire. There is something about birdcages—an intrinsic element of whimsy, perhaps—that continues to spark the creative imagination to higher and higher flights of fancy.

Some of the best cages were wrought by itinerant craftsmen, who imbued their creations with an unbridled sense of whimsy. With its trunklike shape and "studding," a relatively simple cage takes on the look of a treasure chest rescued from the ocean floor. Its cutout handles resemble leaping dolphins.

ORNAMENTAL EXTRAVAGANCE

By the eighteenth century, the making of birdcages had become a noble craft, thanks largely to the growing fashion for bird-keeping. Aristocratic bird fanciers looked for increasingly showy cages, and artisans were more than happy to oblige their demanding patrons. Traditional dome-shaped cages were wildly ornamented with costly and exotic materials. One cage of Sheffield silver plate, topped by an intricate silver crown, is believed to have been commissioned by George III (reigned 1760–1820), but other crowned cages, made for men and women of lesser rank, were equally fantastic.

In addition to excesses of ornamentation, cage-makers experimented with exaggerated and fanciful shapes, to the degree that many birdcages of the eighteenth century no longer resembled cages at all. A French cage in the style of Louis XVI featured sloping concave sides and a bowed front; its decorative finial—a common enough element in cages of the period—was carved to resemble a large goblet out of which rose a fountain of flowers. Not to be outdone by their French brethren, the Dutch produced some highly imaginative cages of their own, including a wood-and-wire cage with carved dentate edges and projections; the roof, with its gilded coat of arms, mimics the silhouette of a crown.

Wickerwork "entertainment centers" were popular during the Victorian era. This one includes a fernery and a graceful arch to support an ample birdcage. The original cage, lost to time and the elements, has been replaced by a contemporary cage with a Victorian feel.

Not surprisingly, the nineteenth century produced a large number of extravagant cages, one of the most spectacular of which is now in the collection of the Cooper-Hewitt Museum. Rumored to have belonged to an Italian queen, it is constructed almost entirely of hand-blown blue Venetian glass, from its elegant dome to its translucent glass bars and its delicate seed and water pots. At once luxurious and understated, the cage has no ornamentation other than a single red silk tassel, which may have served as a plaything for the royal songbirds. Another cage featuring blown glass rods was a highlight of the 1851 Great Exhibition at the Crystal Palace, displayed on a tasseled cushion of blue velvet.

Early-nineteenth-century cages were particularly fanciful, including a Venetian cage whose carved metal ornamentation rises in menacing dentate points, and an oversize cone-shaped cage with brass beading, possibly of northern European origin. As the century waned, cages grew more and more architectural (see Chapter Three), but even these began to feature highly fanciful ornamentation, from miniature flags and Oriental rugs to human figures. A Swedish cage in the collection of decorator Frederika Biggs is topped with a guardhouse and its own diminutive guard, now keeping watch over a large kitchen range.

The bold design of this living room melds seemingly disparate elements like a formal chandelier and a zebra-skin rug. Even in so dramatic a setting, the cage in the window is the center of attention. Looking like a mosque-cum-circus tent, it features such fanciful touches as a looped-metal balcony, castellated trim, and a widow's walk.

FROM GRAND TO MINIATURE

In classical times, the size of the cage indicated the importance of its owner—a principle embraced as well by seventeenth-century men and women of rank who commissioned vast aviaries that housed multiple songbirds. History's most enthusiastic royal bird fancier, the British Charles II (reigned 1660–1685), escaped from the pressures of state by strolling along the avenue where he kept his birds, still known as Bird Cage Walk. A common diversion of the time was to gawk at the king as he fed his pets and attended to their cages, large-scale aviaries designed by the celebrated landscape architect André Lenôtre. Few great estates of the seventeenth and eighteenth centuries were without luxurious aviaries. The Duke of Lauderdale kept "outlandish birds" in a volary in his garden at Ham House, and Strawberry Hill, built for Gothic novelist Horace Walpole, was equipped with a striking Gothic aviary.

Oversize aviaries continued to be popular well into the nineteenth century, from French painted-wood colombiers to storied wire cages that held several families of birds (often equipped with large, twisted branches that served as natural perches). Today, these cages are reproduced in great number; some are tall and rectangular and bring to mind avian condominiums, while others are soaring and pyramidal. An especially handsome tiered cage of the nineteenth century was adorned with wire scroll-work and protruding castellated feeders.

Antique aviaries are still available to the collector, though many command equally overscale prices. An elaborate eight-foot aviary of gilded wood was recently priced at thirty thousand dollars; more modest examples fetch considerably less, though prices rarely fall below four figures. Clearly, these cages make a dramatic statement, and they require an environment of similar scale. Don Black, an antiques buyer for Macy's, remembers a customer who purchased one to fill an empty ballroom.

A plain tabletop becomes center stage with the addition of a spectacular carved birdcage. Fanciful details like tiny wooden bells; a fluid, almost organic dome; and an intricate carved frieze of birds and squirrels enhance the drama—and value—of this one-of-a-kind cage.

In the seventeenth and eighteenth centuries, miniature cages were almost as sought after as grandly scaled aviaries. In the collection of New York's Metropolitan Museum are a three-and-a-half-inch-high German cage of fancifully scrolled silver wire and a tiny English cage of porcelain, less than an inch all around; these cages were obviously intended solely as decoration. Today, minicages are making something of a comeback. Many, such as those sold at Cherishables in Washington, D.C., are designed for use as Christmas tree ornaments. However they are displayed, miniature cages are truly charming.

FLIGHTLESS WONDERS

Even full-size cages weren't always built to house living birds. As early as the fifteenth century, elaborate cages came equipped with stuffed birds, whose filling often included exotic powdered perfumes. In 1751 Lazare Duvaux of Paris sold a small gold cage housing a tiny enamel bird to Madame de Pompadour, and the Marquise du Châtelet boasted a mechanical canary capable of whistling six different tunes. A rage of the eighteenth century was the *serinette*, a mechanical bird that not only sang but hopped from perch to perch on a concealed wire. In the Victorian era, avian automatons reached new heights of mechanical movement, flapping their wings, opening and closing their beaks, and wagging

In nineteenth-century England, the Indian influence was felt in every area of home design, from furniture to upholstery to birdcages. This intricate wirework model was inspired by the Taj Mahal.

their feathered heads from side to side. A gilded cage with a mechanical bird was a popular Victorian wedding gift, the equivalent of today's Crockpot, though infinitely showier.

In addition to mechanical birds, many of these cages included a working clock, either in the base or, if the cage was designed to be hung, underneath it. Munich's Museum of Time Measurement houses a gloriously elaborate eighteenth-century birdcage clock of chased fire-gilt bronze and brass. Two birds inside the cage move their heads, wings, and tail on the hour; their song is provided by a mechanism of twelve miniature flutes. Another fine example of the

Ethereal wirework cages were popular during the nineteenth century, but this model boasts an uncommon element— a spinning "Ferris wheel" that un- doubtedly entertained birds and their human admirers alike.

birdcage clock, probably designed by Robert Adam, hangs from the ceiling of the boudoir at Syon House in Brentford, West London. Like virtually all of these fanciful timepieces, it is richly ornamented, its base painted with opulent flower garlands. In the 1940s a writer for *Country Life* described a similar clock that hung from the ceiling of a Sicilian drawing room; its living inhabitants, he marvelled, seemed entirely unruffled by the loud striking of the hours.

FANTASY CAGES

For sheer whimsy, however, nothing can top the fantasy cages created from the seventeenth century on. If birdcages could be houses, their creators must have mused, why not trains and ships and lion's cages as well? The Venetian bridge described earlier has been extolled as a masterpiece of birdcage building. Equally impressive is an eighteenth-century French cage in the shape of a circus wagon; atop four axled wheels, it is decorated with loops and braids of wire.

The creation of wildly imaginative cages didn't end with the nineteenth century. Taking their inspiration from artisans of the past, twentieth-century cage-makers have come up with all manner of whimsical and surprising forms, from Memphis-style aviaries to converted television sets. Even as the fashion for bird-keeping has waned, the passion to elaborate on the birdcage form continues to soar.

This gilded Chippendale cage is pure fantasy, combining pagoda roofs with gothic gargoyles and Renaissance-style heraldic statuettes. Its startling ornamentation and imposing presence befit the room's grand scale.

Chapter Five

THE
TWENTIETH
CENTURY

y the turn of the century, the birdcage had become not just the focal
point of the Victorian parlor but an
emblem of happy domesticity. This was the era of the
mass-manufactured cage. Companies like Hendryx
of New Haven and Jewett & Company of Buffalo
produced fanciful painted-tin cages by the hundreds
to satisfy the growing market. These were by necessity simpler than the grand architectural cages of the
nineteenth century, but what they lacked in structural
embellishment they made up for in eye-catching
color. Many of these early-twentieth-century cages
have survived, and those that retain traces of their
original paint (now weathered to a soft luster) are
most valued by collectors.

Though mass production dominated the market,
folk artists were still creating extraordinary one-of-
a-kind cages. Tramp-art cages of whittled wood,

*Bird lovers in the early part of the cen-
tury had the option of hanging this
footed cage or setting it atop a table. In a
Manhattan bedroom, it adds a wel-
come sense of the out-of-doors.*

wrought by anonymous but ingenious rural crafts-men from the 1880s through the 1940s, often in-corporated found objects, from old coffee cans to cut-glass "diamonds"; these whimsical expressions of the American spirit are highly collectible today. Other folk-art cages—a tin carousel and a wood-and-wire Ferris wheel, for example—resemble elaborate toys with working parts.

ONWARD AND UPWARD

By the 1920s, however, factory-produced cages had eclipsed the rest of the market. Manufacturers slowly abandoned tin cages for brass, which were not only more durable but easier to keep clean. The new-fashioned cages often included a tall stand, adding an appealing sense of verticality to a room while keep-ing the birds safely away from the family cat. The stands usually included round or half-round hoops from which the cages were suspended, although one popular model featured a pagoda-like top and a stand that echoed the pagoda shape.

The emerging Art Deco style also made itself felt in birdcages of the twenties and thirties. Tall, tiered cages, some of them resembling miniature sky-scrapers, were dramatically *moderne*. Such a cage might serve as the centerpiece of an Art Deco entry-way, or stand as one of several cages in special "bird rooms." A 1931 issue of *House & Garden* included a

A parrot keeps a proprietary eye on an extraordinary oversized cage designed by Patrick Nagar. Frank Lloyd Wright himself might have conceived this clean-lined aviary, which bears a striking resemblance to Wright's own design for the Guggenheim Museum.

design for one such room, with two large aviaries flanking a small pool, in the center of which was— what else?—a bird-shaped fountain. For those Depression-era homeowners who could afford the luxury of a room devoted solely to birds, Katzenbach & Warren offered birdcage-patterned wallpaper in a variety of dramatic colors.

THE AGE OF FUNCTION

Contemporary cages often make a statement, as in sculptor Howard Rosenthal's unique "bird environ-ment"—a disemboweled television set equipped with dowels, swings, and water and seed trays.

In the thirties and forties, companies like Hendryx began producing reproductions of period cages, which included such luxurious accents as mahogany stands and crystal drops. Nevertheless, the guiding principle of the day was practicality—a principle as evident in the manufacture of birdcages as in the production of wartime munitions. Plastic cages— cheap, relatively durable, and eminently easy to

Cage designs of the twentieth century are as varied as its interior styles. This all-purpose room is the perfect setting for a neatly proportioned early-twentieth century model.

maintain—made their appearance in great numbers. (Collectors looking for older cages hospitable to birds have driven up the price of these plastic models in recent years.) For the next quarter century, inexpensive, scrubbable, mass-produced models supplanted all but a very few luxuriously decorated cages. The ornamental cage seemed doomed to extinction, a quaint anachronism as irrelevant to modern life as the antimacassar.

CONTEMPORARY TRENDS

Some of these reproductions are very good indeed. John Rosselli, a New York antiques dealer who specialized in period cages before designing his own line of reproductions, produces elegant and historically inspired models, from a simple English dome-

A large vertical aviary, painted in neon brights, adds drama to a sheltered garden, but the clever addition of wheels allows its owner to move it indoors when foul weather threatens. The rough-hewn wooden branch-perch inside was a popular fixture in ornate eighteenth- and nineteenth-century aviaries.

topped cage to an elegant floor-standing obelisk and a rustic wooden gazebo.

The cage-maker's art, however, is by no means moribund. The fashion for cages has spawned a new generation of artisans and designers whose work rivals the best of previous centuries. Some, like Pat Martinek, take their cue from history. The Dallas-based designer draws on her background as an antiques dealer to create original cages with a period feel. Other artisans use history more directly: Lexington Gardens, a New York shop, offers new cages fancifully recycled from old.

History figures in the work of Eric Lansdown as well, though his cages don't pretend to be reproduction-anything. The San Francisco native specializes in large-scale architectural aviaries whose exquisite details—from mansard roofs and Gothic windows to trompe l'oeil ivy and crumbling bricks—are often whimsically mixed and matched to produce architectural "models" of buildings that exist only in the designer's imagination.

A different architectural slant is evident in the birdcage conceived by Texas designer Mark Osborne. Osborne's fascination with rural architecture—in particular the verticality of old barns—led him to study their shape. Perhaps because he once raised finches, he started to see the barn's half timbers as the diagonal and vertical slats of a birdcage. Now marketed by Joint Venture in Design, this cage model comes in several different finishes.

A fancy for birds and a love of architecture also inspired Belmont Freeman. Now an architect, Freeman was moved to design his first cage as an undergraduate studying suspension bridges. With financial help from the Innovative Design Fund, he created the prototypes for three streamlined cages.

Sculptor Howard Rosenthal's unique cage seems an especially appropriate contemporary symbol. His "bird environment" is nothing more than a collection of dowels, swings, a light, and water and food bins installed inside a disemboweled television set.

What place does a birdcage occupy on the cusp of a new century? It may no longer be a measure of status as it was in senatorial Rome or the Middle Ages; it may no longer evoke the exotic as it did during the Renaissance. But it certainly adds a sense of light and air and grace to a room. It allows each of us, in this age of noise and speed and diminishing space, to be the lord of our own diminutive manor.

San Francisco artist Eric Lansdown is known for his intricate architectural dollhouses and aviaries. The Ivory Palace, above, was inspired by England's Brighton Pavilion, itself a fanciful architectural confection.

A NOTE TO COLLECTORS

*A*ntique birdcages have soared in popularity since the early 1980s, and so, of course, have their prices. At that time, an architectural cage of nineteenth-century vintage might have sold for five hundred dollars in a good antiques store; today the same cage could fetch two thousand dollars. Some early nineteenth-century cages carry price tags of twelve thousand to twenty-five thousand dollars and more, and an extravagantly ornamented cage from the eighteenth century could command upward of fifty thousand dollars at auction. Even prices for the more common mass-manufactured cages from the twenties, thirties, and forties have skyrocketed. In the mid-1980s, they were a common sight at flea markets, going for ten to twenty dollars (and even less if they were missing a tray); today these same cages sell for two hundred fifty dollars and up, and are a great deal harder to find.

If price is no object, an auction house is as good a place as any for one-of-a-kind antique cages. But for the thriftier collector, imagination and perseverance

Finishes add to a cage's collectibility. This contemporary design simulates the veneer of long use with an artificially rusted finish.

are the order of the day. Interesting cages often turn up at small, out-of-the-way shops, which may not charge as much as large, upscale establishments. And they can still be found—though not as easily—at flea markets across America and around the world. (The Paris flea market, for example, continues to be a good source, no doubt because the French have always been such prodigious cage-makers.)

Another effect of the demand for antique cages is a booming market for reproductions—and many of the reproductions are stunningly good. It is, alas, very easy to be taken in by them, though there *are* things a collector can do to make this less likely. First, of course, is to arm oneself with knowledge. By all means, shop around and see what's out there. Most dealers—though not all—are honest about which cages are and are not authentic, and you'll begin to become familiar with the reproductions.

Price is sometimes an indicator of authenticity. If a highly ornamented cage is going for only a few hundred dollars, it is almost certainly a reproduction. (Unfortunately, there have been instances of unscrupulous dealers asking thousands of dollars for "antique" cages that were manufactured several months earlier in Mexico or the Philippines.)

Material is another indicator: Jean Voight, an antiques dealer in Charlottesville, Virginia, advises collectors to be especially wary of bamboo cages marketed as authentic, since few old bamboo cages

Domed wooden cages were popular during the nineteenth century, but many of the models available today are clever reproductions; collectors be wary.

have survived in one piece. According to Howard Kaplan, the quality of the paint can be an important aid in determining whether a birdcage is genuinely antique. On older cages, the paint is almost always worn, a look that many reproductions seek to mimic. But on most reproductions the paint has a smeary look, as if it had been brushed on and then partially wiped off while still wet. The paint on an antique cage, though often chipped or faded, has an appealingly weathered patina. (If the cage you buy *is* an original, this time-worn paint is an asset, and shouldn't be removed unless absolutely necessary.)

As with any sort of collecting, the more you know, the better off you are. The experienced collector develops an instinct for the real thing. Howard Kaplan compares it to the ability to distinguish between a great painting and a mediocre copy. "The real ones," he says, "have a kind of *spirit* about them that the reproductions just don't."

And a final caveat to bird owners: antique cages, while beautiful, are often inhospitable to living pets. The paint almost certainly contains lead, and many of the cages have bent or loose wires that can be extremely sharp. If you're looking for a cage to house live birds, choose one of the new or reproduction cages that were built with bird safety in mind.

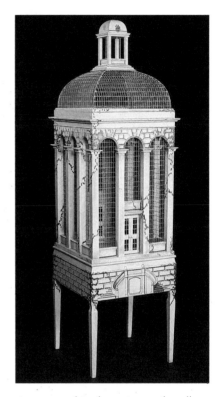

A cage need not be antique to be collectible: Witness this intricate mansard-roof model crafted by Eric Lansdown.

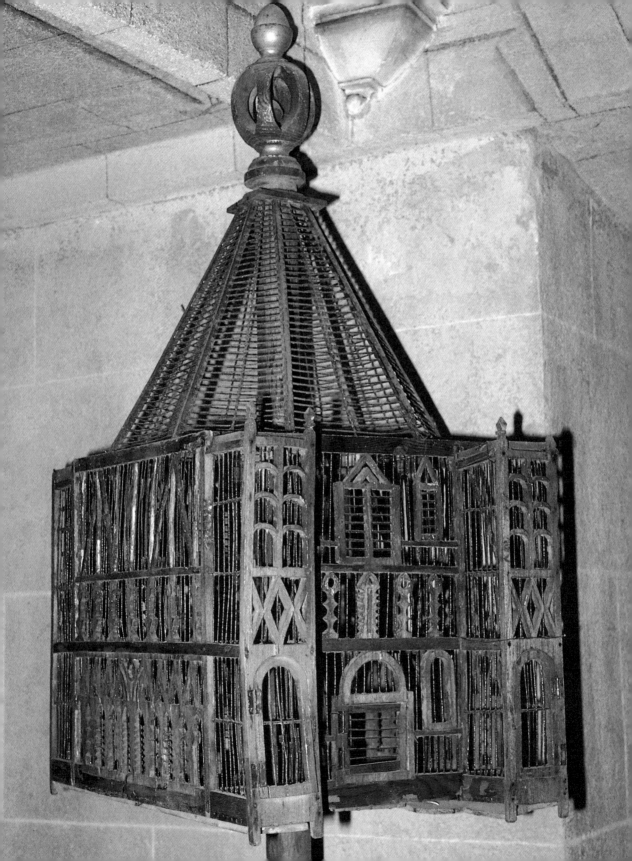

SOURCES

ANTIQUE CAGES

ABC CARPET & HOME
888 Broadway, 2nd floor
New York, NY 10003
212-473-3000
Vintage French, English, and
American cages.

BETTY JANE BART ANTIQUES
1225 Madison Avenue
New York, NY 10128
212-410-2702
Wide selection of antique
cages, from basic to highly
ornamental.

CHERISHABLES
1608 20th Street N.W.
Washington, DC 20009
202-785-3616
Nineteenth- and early
twentieth-century architectural
cages; also new miniature cage
ornaments.

CORNER HOUSE ANTIQUES
Main Street and Old Mill
Pond Road
Sheffield, MA 01257
413-229-6627
Specializes in Victorian wicker
of all kinds, and usually has
one or two cages and/or stands
on hand. Will try to locate
specific pieces.

DEVONSHIRE
6 North Madison Street
Middleburg, VA 22117
703-687-5990
English Victorian cages. Stores
in Bridgehampton, Palm Beach,
and Newport.

DOVETAILS
511 East Water Street
Charlottesville, VA 22901
804-979-9955
Antique cages, all styles and
periods.

FERRET
12334 Ventura Boulevard
Studio City, CA 91604
818-769-2427
Small selection of one-of-a-kind
cages.

FORD A. KALIL
6822 Wisconsin Avenue
Chevy Chase, MD 20814
301-656-9200
Eighteenth- and nineteenth-
century English and French
cages.

FRENCH CORNER ANTIQUES
130 Coulter Avenue
Ardmore, PA 19003
215-642-6867
Antique French cages in a
variety of styles.

GRASS ROOTS ANTIQUES
12 Main Street North
Woodbury, CT 06798
203-263-3983
Limited selection of antique
cages in a variety of styles.

HOWARD KAPLAN ANTIQUES
827 Broadway
New York, NY 10003
212-677-1000
Nineteenth-century French
cages.

Architect Belmont Freeman applied the engineering principles of suspension bridges to create a series of streamlined
and spectacular birdcages, including this stunning model.

HUBERT DES FORGES
1193 Lexington Avenue
New York, NY 10028
212-744-1857
Nineteenth-century French
cages.

J. GARVIN MECKING
72 East 11th Street
New York, NY 10003
212-677-4316
English and French cages; to
the trade only.

JOHN ROSSELLI
523 East 73rd Street
New York, NY 10021
212-772-2137
English and French cages; to
the trade only.

JONATHAN PETERS
5 Main Street
New Preston, CT 06777
203-868-9017
Antique birdcages from all eras,
including many Hendryx cages.

KEITH SKEEL ANTIQUES
94-98 Islington High Street
London NW1 England
44-71-226-7012
French cages, most from the
mid-nineteenth century.

LEXINGTON GARDENS
1008 Lexington Avenue
New York, NY 10021
212-861-4390
Often carries antique, new, and
reproduction cages; styles and
vintage vary.

LIMITED EDITIONS
253 East 72nd Street
New York, NY 10021
212-249-5563
Period and reproduction cages.

*The use of contrasting paint colors on the door and "window"
of this gabled cage, gives it a particularly fanciful air.*

MACY'S CORNER SHOP
ANTIQUES
151 West 34th Street, 9th floor
New York, NY 10001
212-560-4049
Quality nineteenth-century
cages.

SUSAN PARRISH ANTIQUES
390 Bleecker Street
New York, NY 10014
212-645-5020
American cages, most from the
nineteenth century.

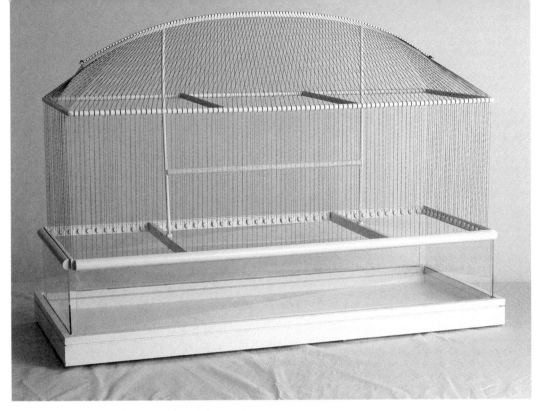

The horizontality of this cage by Belmont Freeman was designed to facilitate flight. It features a thirty-three-inch runway and a domed top.

NEW AND REPRODUCTION CAGES

(See also ABC Carpet & Home, Devonshire, Ferret, John Rosselli, Lexington Gardens, and Limited Editions under Antique Cages.)

GOLDEN OLDIES
132-29 33rd Avenue
Flushing, NY 11354
718-445-4400
Period reproductions.

HAT & THE HEART
2806 East Madison
Seattle, WA 98112
206-325-9909
American antique and
reproduction cages.

LA RUCHE
174 Newbury Street
Boston, MA 02116
617-536-6366
Period reproductions, new designs.

PAINTING WITH FLOWERS
298 Main Street
Port Washington, NY 11050
516-883-4164
Mostly reproduction cages.

POTTERY BARN
Mail Order Department
P.O. Box 7044
San Francisco, CA 94120
415-421-3400
Reproductions of Victorian
cages.

TERRA COTTA
11925 Montana Avenue
Los Angeles, CA 90049
213-826-7878
Occasionally antique, but
mostly reproduction cages.

UMBRELLO
8607 Melrose Avenue
Los Angeles, CA 90069
213-659-4335
Small selection of
Mexican cages.

WHOLESALERS
AND IMPORTERS

Many of the following
companies will provide the
names of retailers that carry
their cages.

THE CULTIVATED
GARDEN INC.
259 Fourth Street
Hoboken, NJ 07030
201-656-3564
Victorian-style wood-and-wire
cages.

OAK SMITH & JONES
1321 Second Avenue
New York, NY 10021
212-535-1451
Occasionally antique, but
mostly reproduction cages.

THE DESIGN COLLECTION
3844 West Northside Drive
Jackson, MS 39209
601-366-4229
Mexican wire cages.

GUANGDONG
CERAMICS, INC.
716 Monterey Pass Road
Monterey Park, CA 91754
213-268-9883
Chinese cages.

ISADORA & MIZRAHI
225 Fifth Avenue
New York, NY 10010
800-542-8689
Contemporary and
reproduction birdcages.

KELVIN CHEN
INTERNATIONAL
14838 Valley Boulevard
City of Industry, CA 91746
818-961-7828
Good selection of Chinese
cages.

KUNISON INTERNATIONAL
5415 Argosy Drive
Huntington Beach, CA 92649
714-898-3386
Rustic bent-twig cages.

POLLY LIN ORIENTAL ARTS
The L.A. Mart
1933 South Broadway
Los Angeles, CA 90007
213-749-9474
Chinese cages.

A beautiful white cage with a radiating-spoke center conjures up images of the ferris wheel carnival ride.

ROSENTHAL- NETTER
11311 Roosevelt Boulevard
Philadelphia, PA 19154
215-464-2200
Original designs in rattan,
metal, teak, and bamboo
from Indonesia, China, and
the Philippines.

WOODENWORKS
1201 North 4th Street
Watertown, WI 53094
414-261-2445
Reproduction cages in wood
and wire.

CRAFTSPEOPLE
AND DESIGN FIRMS

BELMONT FREEMAN
212-382-3311
Custom-built tension-wire
cages of sculptural quality.

JOINT VENTURE IN DESIGN
800-627-5238
Barn-style birdcage, designed
by Mark Osborne, in a variety
of finishes.

ERIC LANSDOWN
415-822-1325
Architectural aviaries and
custom cages.

PHOTO CREDITS

Rick Albert, courtesy of Motif
Designs, 77
Peter Bosch, 35
© Bob Braun, 91
Nick Carter/EWA, 12
Tony Cenicola, 21, 24, 33, 34,
37, 53, 54, 69, 74, 88
The Cultivated Garden Inc., 17,
49
Design Collection, a division of
Country Originals, Inc., 25,
27, 80
Bill Emberley, 6, 72, 79, 83
© Phillip H. Ennis, 62, 67, 71
Courtesy of Gardener's Eden,
36
Courtesy of Hammacher
Schlemmer, 45
David Hamsley, 73, 87, 89
Mark Hill, 11, 16, 20, 28, 30,
41, 52, 64, 65
Lizzie Himmel, 50, 75
Courtesy of Joint Venture in
Design, 29
© Jenifer Jordan, 32
© Annie Kelly, 18
© Karen Kent, 3, 6

© Steven Klahr, 23, 82
© Elyse Lewin, 47, 61, 68
Oleg March, 8
Jeff McNamara, 15
Mikos of Jesse Walker Assoc.,
57
Courtesy of Palecek, 43
© David Phelps, 59
© David Phelps, from *Formal
Country* by Pat Ross,
published by Viking Studio
Books, 51
Courtesy of Pottery Barn, 44
© Lanny Provo, 6, 7
© Maria Robledo, 70
Howard Rosenthal, 76
Courtesy of Herbert Schiffer
Antiques, 38, 39
© Walter Smalling, 31, 40, 58,
63
© Tim Street-Porter, 26, 78
Marianne Sullivan, 19
Elizabeth Whiting &
Associates, 42
Lillian Williams, 55, 56, 84
Peter Woloszynski/EWA, 85

INDEX

References to captions are written in italic type.